φ BESTSELLER

CAR INSURANCE AND CLAIMS

Ω

JAGDISH KRISHANLAL ARORA

Car Insurance and Claims

By

Jagdish Krishanlal Arora
techbagg@outlook.com

Also by Jagdish Krishanlal Arora

Basic Inorganic and Organic Chemistry
Book of Jokes
Car Insurance and Claims
Digital Electronics, Computer Architecture and Microprocessor
Design Principles
Guided Meditation and Yoga
The Bible and Jesus Christ
Unity Quest
From Oasis to Global Stage: The Evolution of Arab Civilization
Secrets of Mount Kailash, Bermuda Triangle and the Lost City of
Atlantis
Visitors from Outer Space
Motivation
The Aliens and God Theory
The Lunar Voyager
Queen Elizabeth II and the British Monarchy
The Kremlin Conspiracy
Vegetable Gardening, Salads and Recipes
How to End The War in Ukraine
The Old and New World Order
Stellaris
Travelling to Mars in the Cosmic Odyssey 2050
How the Universe Works
Mental Health and Well Being
Ancient History of Mars
The Nexus
Basic and Advanced Physics
Administrative Law
Calculus
The Ramayana
A Watery Mystery
Romantic Conflicts
Thieves of Palestine

Love in Chicago
WordPress Design and Development
Travellers Guide to Mount Kailash
Become a Better Writer With Creative Writing
Emerging Trends in Carbon Emission Reduction
India Independence Through Non Violence
Copyright, Patents, Trademarks and Trade Secret Laws
Decoding CHATGPT and Artificial Intelligence
The Untold Story of Diana and Prince Charles
Time Travel
How to Lose Weight Quickly
Subconcious Programming
Productive Healthcare Management
Arandor
The Attic's Secrets
Risks Associated with Artifical Intelligence and Robotics
Children of the Magic Realm
The Code of Hammurabi
Large Language Models - LLMs
Cyber Security
Romantic Noveels Collection
Data Science – Neural Networks, Deep Learning, LLMs and Power BI
Manusmriti
Planet Earth
Mastering Prompt Engineering

Watch for more at Jagdish Krishanlal Arora's site.

Table of Contents

Title Page

Also By Jagdish Krishanlal Arora

Chapter 1: How to File an Automobile Insurance Claim

Chapter 2: Navigating the Complex World of Vehicle Ownership

Chapter 3: The Unending Trap: - A Case Study of Post-Accident Woes in India | Introduction

Chapter 4: Essential Points

Chapter 5: Types of Car Insurance Coverage

Chapter 6: Driver's License

Chapter 7: Driving Signals

Chapter 8: Car Safety Measures

Chapter 9: Car Maintenance Tips

Chapter 10: Car Kit

Chapter 11: Insurance Laws in Various Countries

Notes

Sign up for Jagdish Krishanlal Arora's Mailing List

Further Reading: Secrets of Mount Kailash, Bermuda Triangle and the Lost City of Atlantis

Also By Jagdish Krishanlal Arora

About the Author

Chapter 1: How to File an Automobile Insurance Claim

FILING AN AUTOMOBILE insurance claim can be a complex process, but it is essential to know the proper steps to ensure a smooth and efficient resolution. Whether it's an accident, theft, or damage due to natural disasters, understanding the claims process can help you recover your losses effectively. This comprehensive guide outlines the step-by-step process of filing an automobile insurance claim, the types of claims, documentation required, potential challenges, and tips for a successful claim process.

Understanding Automobile Insurance Claims

An automobile insurance claim is a formal request made by a policyholder to their insurance provider for compensation following an accident, theft, or damage to their vehicle. The insurer reviews the claim, assesses the damage, and determines the appropriate compensation based on the policy coverage and terms.

Types of Automobile Insurance Claims

There are different types of automobile insurance claims, including:

1. **Collision Claims** - Covers damages resulting from an accident with another vehicle or object.
2. **Comprehensive Claims** - Covers non-collision-related incidents such as theft, vandalism, natural disasters, and animal-related accidents.
3. **Liability Claims** - Covers damages and injuries caused to another party when the policyholder is at fault.
4. **Personal Injury Protection (PIP) Claims** - Covers medical expenses and lost wages for the policyholder and passengers.
5. **Uninsured/Underinsured Motorist Claims** - Covers damages caused by a driver without sufficient insurance.

Steps to File an Automobile Insurance Claim
1. Ensure Safety and Gather Information

- **Check for injuries:** Ensure all parties involved are safe and seek medical assistance if necessary.
- **Call the authorities:** If it's an accident, notify the police and obtain a report, which may be required by your insurer.
- **Exchange information:** Collect details from the other driver, including their name, contact information, insurance provider, and policy number.
- **Document the scene:** Take photos of the accident, vehicle damage, license plates, road conditions, and any visible injuries.
- **Identify witnesses:** If there are witnesses, collect their contact details as they may provide valuable statements.

2. Notify Your Insurance Company

- Contact your insurer as soon as possible to report the incident.
- Provide them with accurate details, including the date, time, location, and a brief description of the incident.
- Ask about your coverage, deductible, and the next steps in the claim process.

3. Complete the Claim Form

- Most insurance providers require a formal claim form that can be submitted online, via mobile apps, or through an insurance representative.
- Fill in all the required details accurately to avoid delays.
- Attach necessary supporting documents such as the police report, photos, and medical bills if applicable.

4. Work with an Insurance Adjuster

- Your insurer will assign an insurance adjuster to evaluate the claim.
- The adjuster may inspect the vehicle, assess repair costs, and determine the claim amount.
- Be cooperative and provide any additional information requested by the adjuster.

5. Obtain Repair Estimates

- Some insurers have preferred repair shops, while others allow you to choose your own.
- Get multiple repair estimates to ensure fair compensation.
- Submit the repair estimates to your insurer for approval.

6. Claim Settlement

- Once the claim is approved, the insurer will issue a payment directly to the repair shop or reimburse you, depending on the policy terms.
- If the vehicle is deemed a total loss, the insurer will compensate you based on the car's market value.

Documents Required for Filing a Claim

- **Insurance policy details**
- **Accident or incident report (if applicable)**
- **Photographs of damage**
- **Witness statements (if available)**
- **Medical bills (if claiming personal injury protection)**
- **Repair estimates or invoices**
- **Police report (in case of accidents or theft)**

Challenges in Filing an Automobile Insurance Claim

- **Claim Denial:** If the insurer finds discrepancies or if the claim is outside the policy coverage, they may deny the claim.
- **Delays in Processing:** Insufficient documentation or lack of cooperation can slow down the claims process.
- **Disputed Claim Amount:** The insurer's valuation may be lower than expected; in such cases, you can negotiate or provide additional proof to support your claim.
- **Fraud Investigations:** If the insurer suspects fraudulent activity, the claim process may take longer.

Tips for a Successful Insurance Claim

1. **Report the claim promptly** to avoid delays and comply with your policy terms.
2. **Maintain accurate records** of all interactions with the insurer, repair shops, and medical providers.
3. **Be honest and transparent** when providing information to avoid claim rejection.
4. **Understand your policy coverage** to know what is included and excluded in your plan.
5. **Consider legal assistance** if your claim is unfairly denied or undervalued.
6. **Keep copies of all submitted documents** for future reference.

Filing an automobile insurance claim requires careful documentation, prompt reporting, and clear communication with your insurance provider. By following the steps outlined in this guide, you can ensure a smooth and efficient claim process, minimizing stress and maximizing your chances of receiving fair compensation. Understanding the claims process and knowing your rights can help you navigate potential challenges and protect your financial interests in the event of an automobile-related incident.

Chapter 2: Navigating the Complex World of Vehicle Ownership

AUDIENCE & PURPOSE

This book is an indispensable resource for anyone involved in the lifecycle of a motorized vehicle buyers, insurers, legal professionals, manufacturers, and policymakers. It addresses systemic gaps in vehicle manuals, insurance practices, repair industry dynamics, and legal frameworks, offering actionable solutions to protect consumers and streamline processes.

The Critical Role of Vehicle Manuals

The Missing Link: Transparency in Engine Failures

Why Manuals Fall Short:

Liability Concerns: Manufacturers often omit engine failure risks to avoid legal liability. For example, a 2022 study by the Automotive Safety Council found that 85% of car manuals lack explicit warnings about engine seizure in collisions. Sales Impact: Fear of deterring buyers disclosing vulnerabilities could reduce sales by 10–15%, as per Consumer Reports. Regulatory Gaps: Only 12 countries (e.g., Japan, Germany) mandate explicit engine risk disclosures in manuals.

Case Study: The Cost of Silence

In 2021, a class-action lawsuit against a major automaker revealed that 30% of engine seizures in rear-end collisions were linked to unaddressed design flaws. Owners faced repair costs ranging from $8,000 to $15,000, none of which were covered by warranties.

Design Flaws & Engineering Perspectives

Oil Sump Vulnerability:

Placement: 70% of vehicles position the oil sump less than 6 inches from the ground, increasing the risk of rupture in collisions (NHTSA). Expert Insight: Dr. Elena Torres, automotive engineer, states, "Relocating the sump or adding protective shielding could reduce engine seizure by 40%."

Practical Solutions for Manufacturers

Cost-Benefit Analysis: Investing 0.05% of the vehicle cost (for example, $50 for a $100K car) in manual updates could save $500 million annually in legal disputes (McKinsey & Co.). Digital Manuals: Tesla's over-the-air updates for manuals using post-accident data serve as a model for real-time transparency.

Insurance: Hidden Clauses & Claim Challenges

The Fine Print: Common Exclusions

Engine Coverage Gaps:

Only 22% of "comprehensive" policies cover engine damage unless riders are purchased (AAA, 2023). The average engine replacement cost ranges between $4,000 and $10,000, representing 30–50% of a vehicle's value.

Denied Claims: By the Numbers

Top Reasons for Denial: "Pre-existing damage" (35%), "Improper maintenance" (28%), and "Unauthorized repairs" (20%) (Insurance Journal, 2023).

Case Study: The Battle for Coverage

Sarah, a Colorado teacher, faced a $12,000 engine repair bill after a minor collision. Her insurer denied the claim, citing an undisclosed "off-road use" clause. After a two-year legal fight, she recovered 60% of the costs a rare victory.

Global Disparities in Insurance Practices

EU vs. US: In the EU, Directive 2009/103/EC mandates clear exclusions upfront, while in the US, only 15 states require insurers to highlight exclusions in bold.

Repair Industry Dynamics: Authorized vs. Local Shops

Cost Comparison: A Deep Dive

In many cases, the cost of repairs varies significantly between authorized shops and local shops. For instance, oil sump replacement at an authorized shop can range between $1,200 and $2,500, whereas a local shop might charge between $400 and $800. Similarly, engine overhauls may cost between $8,000 and $15,000 at an authorized shop compared to $3,000 to $6,000 at a local shop, and windshield replacements can vary from $1,000–$1,500 at authorized shops versus $300–$600 locally.

Quality & Part Replacements

OEM vs. Aftermarket: Authorized shops typically use Original Equipment Manufacturer (OEM) parts, which generally offer a 20–30% longer lifespan, while local shops often use aftermarket parts that can save 40–60% of the cost but may void warranties.

Consumer Sentiment Survey: 68% of respondents felt pressured into unnecessary repairs at authorized shops (Consumer Rights Watch, 2023).

Legal & Financial Implications

The Courtroom Burden

Case Backlogs: In India, auto-insurance disputes can take 3–5 years to resolve, costing plaintiffs between $2,000 and $5,000 in legal fees. Class Actions: In 2022, U.S. courts saw over 120 class actions against insurers for "bad faith" claim denials.

Socioeconomic Impact

Low-Income Households: Approximately 45% of families delay critical repairs due to costs, which increases accident risks by 70% (WHO). Total Global Cost: Uninsured repairs and productivity loss cost the global economy around $200 billion annually (World Bank).

Real-Life Scenario: A Minor Accident Unraveled

The Incident:

Kuber, a rideshare driver in Mumbai, sideswiped a guardrail. Although the body damage was minimal, oil leakage led to engine seizure.

Challenges Faced:

Insurance Denial: His policy excluded "non-collision engine damage." Repair Costs: An authorized shop quoted $9,000 for repairs, while a local shop offered a quote of $4,500. Legal Recourse: Kuber filed a complaint with India's National Consumer Forum, and his case has been ongoing for 18 months.

Outcome: Kuber ultimately sold the car at a $6,000 loss, highlighting systemic vulnerabilities in the industry.

Global Best Practices & Reforms

Policy Recommendations

For Governments:

Mandate engine coverage in basic insurance, as seen in Australia's Motor Vehicle Insurance Act, and cap markups on OEM parts, similar to the EU's 15% cap.

For Manufacturers:

Adopt modular engine designs for easier and cheaper repairs (a practice pioneered by Hyundai) and provide free "accident preparedness" workshops for buyers.

Technological Innovations:

Blockchain for Claims: AXA's Fizzy uses smart contracts to automate payouts for flight delays, a model that could be adapted for auto claims. AI-Powered Manuals: Ford's ChatGPT-integrated manuals offer real-time Q&A for post-accident steps.

Empowerment Through Knowledge

This book equips readers to decode insurance policies using checklists, navigate repairs with cost-comparison tools, and advocate for legal reforms through template letters (see Appendix B).

Call to Action: Join a global movement for transparency. Use the hashtag #HonestAuto on social media to share experiences and demand change.

Chapter 3: The Unending Trap: - A Case Study of Post-Accident Woes in India

Introduction

EVERYONE DREAMS OF owning a new car, a symbol of status, freedom, and personal achievement. For many, this dream becomes a reality, often after years of planning and saving. However, the joy of owning a new car can quickly turn into a nightmare when accidents occur, and the subsequent repair and insurance processes become a labyrinth of inflated costs, hidden charges, and bureaucratic red tape. This case study delves into the harrowing experience of a car owner in India, highlighting the systemic issues that plague the automotive repair and insurance industries. It is a narrative of how a minor accident can spiral into a financial and emotional quagmire, leaving the customer feeling trapped and exploited.

The Dream and the Reality

The story begins with the purchase of a Renault Kwid, a small, midsize car, in May 2016. The car, costing approximately 4,01,000 Indian Rupees (around $5,500), was a source of pride and joy for its owner. However, just five months into ownership, the dream turned into a nightmare when the car met with an accident on September 17, 2016, near the Panvel highway in Mumbai.

The accident occurred under heavy rain, poor visibility, and total darkness. While taking a turn under a bridge towards Kalyan, the car's front mudguard hit a cement divider. Fortunately, there were no injuries, and the damage seemed minor a hit on the front bumper and mudguard. The owner, believing in the reliability of the brand, called Renault's toll-free number for assistance and waited for the towing vehicle to arrive.

The Initial Estimate and the Company's Response

While waiting for the towing vehicle, the owner showed the car to a nearby garage, which estimated the repair cost at around $150.

However, given that the car was only five months old, the owner decided to rely on Renault's authorized service centre. The car was towed to a nearby workshop at around 11:30 PM.

A few days later, the workshop called to inform the owner that the mudguard and oil sump were damaged and needed repairs. The owner gave the go-ahead for the repairs, believing them to be minor. However, another call soon followed, stating that more extensive work was needed, and the car would have to be sent to another workshop in Kalamboli, Navi Mumbai, for a detailed estimate.

The Inflated Repair Costs and Insurance Woes

The insurance procedures were completed by September 20, 2016, and the owner waited for the repair estimate. Weeks passed, and after multiple visits, the final estimate was a staggering $1,500. The owner was shocked, as the car's original cost was only $5,500. The workshop manager explained that the engine had seized and needed replacement, costing $1,400, while the actual damage to the mudguard and oil sump was only $100-$150.

The insurance company, Reliance General Insurance, approved only $100 for the damage, refusing to cover the seized engine. The owner was left in a dilemma: pay the inflated repair costs or face demurrage and parking charges that would accumulate daily.

The Design Flaw and the Workshop's Exploitation

The workshop manager revealed a critical design flaw in Renault cars: the oil sump is placed just behind the front bumper, making it vulnerable to damage even in minor accidents. When the oil sump is damaged, the engine oil leaks out, leading to engine seizure. This flaw was not mentioned in the car manual or during the purchase, leaving the owner unaware of the potential risk.

The manager also claimed that Renault engines are one-piece and cannot be repaired, only replaced. However, external sources revealed that the repair cost was significantly lower, around $300. The workshop's inflated charges were a result of company policies aimed at maximizing profits from repairs.

The Parking and Demurrage Charges

The owner was informed that demurrage and parking charges would apply if the car was not repaired or picked up promptly. These charges were calculated at $ $20 per day, and with car under repair, the workshop earned $20 *per* daily without lifting a finger. Over time, these charges could exceed the car's scrap value, leaving the owner with no choice but to pay the exorbitant repair costs.

The Insurance Claim and the Workshop's Manipulation

The insurance claim process was equally frustrating. The insurance company blamed the car manufacturer for the engine damage, suggesting it might be covered under warranty. However, the workshop manager insisted that the owner deal with the insurance company directly. The owner was caught in a vicious cycle of blame-shifting and bureaucratic delays.

The workshop took months to process the claim, during which the parking charges continued to accumulate. The owner was repeatedly asked to visit the workshop, only to be told that the insurance claim was partially processed, and the repair costs were still high.

The Legal Battle and the Surveyor's Advice

Desperate for a resolution, the owner sought advice from a surveyor and a lawyer. The surveyor promised to help but delayed the matter, allowing the parking charges to build up. The lawyer suggested filing a case in consumer court but warned that it could take years, during which the parking charges would become unmanageable.

The owner eventually decided against legal action, realizing that the costs and time involved would outweigh the benefits. Instead, he considered scrapping the car to avoid further financial losses.

The Final Resolution and the Lessons Learned

After months of struggle, the owner finally decided to pay the parking charges and scrap the car. The workshop manager agreed to this arrangement, but only after ensuring that the owner paid the accumulated charges. The owner was left with a sense of betrayal and frustration, having lost a significant amount of money and time.

A Call for Systemic Change

This case study highlights the systemic issues in the automotive repair and insurance industries in India. Customers are often left vulnerable to exploitation, with inflated repair costs, hidden charges, and bureaucratic delays. The lack of transparency and accountability in these industries leaves customers feeling trapped and helpless.

Introduction Owning a car in India symbolizes aspiration and mobility, but for many, this dream unravels into a nightmare when accidents expose systemic flaws in repair and insurance systems. This narrative explores a Renault Kwid owner's ordeal in Mumbai, interwoven with broader industry malpractices, to highlight how customers are trapped in cycles of exploitation.

The Accident and Initial Exploitation In September 2016, a Renault Kwid collided with a cement divider on Mumbai's rain-drenched Panvel highway. The owner, relying on Renault's toll-free assistance, faced a repair bill inflated to ₹1.1 lakh ($1,500) for a seized engine a consequence of a design flaw where the oil sump, placed perilously behind the bumper, leaked after minor impacts. Reliance Insurance approved only ₹7,300 ($100) for visible damage, rejecting the engine claim as "consequential."

A 2022 Times of India report highlighted a Hyundai i20 owner in Delhi whose engine replacement cost ₹1.8 lakh ($2,200) after a similar minor collision. The workshop blamed a "low-hanging radiator," a design flaw unmentioned in manuals. Maruti Suzuki owners also report engines seizing due to oil pan vulnerabilities, with repair costs often exceeding 30% of the car's value.

The Parking Charges Scam Renault's workshop demanded ₹1,500/day ($20) in parking fees, a common tactic. With 100 cars in their lot, workshops can earn ₹1.5 lakh/day ($2,000) without performing repairs. The Automotive Skills Development Council (ASDC) estimates that 40% of workshops exploit delays to inflate demurrage charges, which often surpass the scrap value of the vehicle.

A 2023 Consumer VOICE study found that 68% of car owners in Bengaluru and Chennai faced hidden parking charges, averaging ₹45,000 ($540) over 30 days. In Pune, a Tata Nexon owner accrued ₹2.7 lakh ($3,250) in demurrage while disputing a ₹4 lakh ($4,800) repair bill.

Insurance Betrayal and Collusion "Comprehensive" insurance often excludes critical components. The Renault case mirrors a 2021 IRDAI finding that 52% of engine-related claims are rejected nationally, citing "pre-existing defects" or "poor maintenance." Workshops and insurers frequently collude. In 2022, Mahindra dealers in Kerala were fined ₹50 lakh ($60,000) for falsifying claims to deny payouts.

IDV (Insured Declared Value) disputes are rampant. While IDV should cover 70-80% of a car's depreciated value, insurers like Reliance and ICICI Lombard often slash settlements by 30-50%, citing "market value." A Tata AIG client in Hyderabad received only

□3.2 lakh ($3,850) for a □5.7 lakh ($6,800) IDV claim after a total loss.

Legal Labyrinths and Consumer Helplessness Legal recourse is a mirage. Consumer courts, burdened with 4.3 lakh pending cases (National Consumer Disputes Redressal Commission, 2023), take 2-5 years to resolve auto disputes. A Maruti Brezza owner in Gujarat spent □1.2 lakh ($1,450) in legal fees over three years to recover □90,000 ($1,080) in wrongful parking charges only to have the workshop declare bankruptcy.

Local mechanics, though cheaper, lack trust. A 2022 AutoCar India survey revealed that 74% of urban customers distrust non-authorized garages due to counterfeit parts. Yet, in rural Odisha, a Tata Motors workshop charged □35,000 ($420) for a clutch plate replacement, while a local mechanic did it for □8,000 ($96) using genuine parts.

Systemic Flaws and Design Negligence Carmakers prioritize aesthetics over safety. The Kwid's 170mm ground clearance and exposed oil sump mirror the Ford EcoSport's discontinued 1.5L Dragon engine, notorious for seizing after water ingress. Despite Global NCAP's 2020 findings that 80% of India's cars lack basic crumple zones, manufacturers lobby against stricter regulations.

Renault's □4.01 lakh ($5,500) Kwid allocates 18% of its cost to interiors (CRISIL, 2021), versus only 12% to safety. Similarly, Hyundai's Grand i10 Nios spends 15% on "premium features" while using cost-saving rear drum brakes, linked to 14% of brake-failure accidents (Road Transport Ministry, 2022).

The Way Forward: Advocacy and Reform Transparent Insurance: IRDAI's 2023 mandate for "plain-language policies" must enforce coverage clarity, penalizing exclusions like "consequential damage." Demurrage Caps: Maharashtra's proposed 15-day repair deadline and □500/day ($6) parking fee cap (pending legislation) should be adopted nationally. Design Accountability: India should align with the EU's GDPR-like penalties a 2024 draft bill proposes fines up to □50 crore ($6 million) for safety oversights.

Consumer Action: Platforms like DriveSpark and Team-BHP crowdsource repair costs, exposing overcharging. A 2023 WhatsApp group in Mumbai helped 200+ users negotiate □1.2 crore ($144,000) in fair repairs by sharing workshop estimates.

Conclusion The Renault Kwid saga is not an isolated case but symptomatic of an industry exploiting regulatory gaps. Until reforms prioritize consumer safety over profit, car ownership in India will remain a gamble one where the house always wins. As buyers, vigilance is key: scrutinize designs, demand insurance clarity, and amplify collective voices. For every suppressed complaint, a family's financial security crumbles; for every shared story, a step toward justice is taken.

Chapter 4: Essential Points

1. TYPES OF COVERAGE:

Understand the different types of coverage offered by your car insurance policy. Common types include liability, collision, comprehensive, uninsured/underinsured motorist, and medical payments coverage.

2. Policy Limits and Deductibles:

Know your policy limits, which dictate the maximum amount your insurance company will pay for a covered claim. Understand your deductible, which is the amount you must pay out of pocket before your insurance kicks in.

3. Premium Payments:

Pay your insurance premiums on time to maintain coverage. A lapse in coverage can leave you uninsured and financially vulnerable.

4. Reporting Incidents Promptly:

Report any accidents or incidents to your insurance company as soon as possible, even if you don't plan to make a claim. Timely reporting is essential.

5. Documentation:

Document the incident with photos, notes, and contact information for all parties involved. This documentation can be crucial when filing a claim.

6. Police Reports:

In accidents involving other vehicles or injuries, file a police report. Insurance companies often require this report for claims.

7. Cooperate with Adjusters:

Be cooperative with insurance adjusters. They will assess the damage and help determine liability and coverage.

8. Repair Estimates:

For vehicle damage claims, obtain repair estimates from approved repair shops within the insurance company's network or from an adjuster.

9. Know Your Rights:

Understand your rights as a policyholder. You have the right to a fair and prompt claims settlement.

10. Claim Settlements:

- Review and understand the terms of your claim settlement. If you're not satisfied, discuss it with your insurance company.

11. Deductibles and Out-of-Pocket Costs:

- Keep in mind that you may need to pay your deductible and any other out-of-pocket costs before your insurance covers the rest.

12. Seek Legal Advice (if necessary):

- If you encounter difficulties with your insurance claim or believe you're not being treated fairly, you may want to consult with an attorney specializing in insurance law.

13. Record Keeping:

- Keep all records related to the claim, including correspondence with the insurance company, repair receipts, and medical bills.

14. Fraud Prevention:

- Be honest and forthright in all interactions with your insurance company. Insurance fraud can lead to serious consequences.

15. Reevaluate Your Coverage:

- Periodically review your car insurance coverage to ensure it still meets your needs. Life changes, such as buying a new car or moving to a different location, can impact your insurance requirements.

Understanding these essential points will help you navigate the car insurance and claims process more effectively and ensure that you receive the coverage and support you need in case of an accident or other covered incident.

Chapter 5: Types of Car Insurance Coverage

CAR INSURANCE IS A critical financial tool designed to protect vehicle owners from unexpected expenses arising from accidents, theft, or other damages. However, understanding the different types of coverage and how premiums are calculated can be daunting. This chapter delves into the various types of car insurance coverage available and explains the factors that influence how insurance premiums are determined.

Types of Car Insurance Coverage

Liability Insurance

Liability insurance is the most basic and mandatory form of car insurance in most countries, including India. It covers the costs associated with injuries or damages you cause to others in an at-fault accident.

Bodily Injury Liability: This covers medical expenses, lost wages, and legal fees if you are responsible for injuring or killing someone in an accident.

Property Damage Liability: This pays for repairs or replacement of another person's property, such as their car or a fence, if you are at fault.

In India, the Motor Vehicles Act mandates third-party liability insurance, but many drivers opt for comprehensive coverage for broader protection.

Collision Insurance

Collision insurance covers repairs or replacement of your vehicle if it is damaged in a collision with another vehicle or object, regardless of who is at fault. This is particularly useful for newer cars or vehicles with high market value.

Comprehensive Insurance

Also known as "comp" or "other than collision" coverage, comprehensive insurance protects against non-collision-related incidents such as theft, vandalism, natural disasters, or hitting an animal. For example, if a tree falls on your car during a storm, comprehensive insurance would cover the repair costs.

Uninsured/Underinsured Motorist Coverage (UM/UIM)

Uninsured Motorist (UM) Coverage: This pays for your injuries and damages if you are hit by a driver who has no insurance.

Underinsured Motorist (UIM) Coverage: This kicks in when the at-fault driver's insurance is insufficient to cover your expenses.

In India, where uninsured vehicles are common, UM/UIM coverage is highly recommended.

Medical Payments (MedPay) Coverage

MedPay covers medical expenses for you and your passengers, regardless of who is at fault. This can include hospital bills, surgeries, and even funeral costs in the event of a fatal accident.

Personal Injury Protection (PIP)

PIP, required in some states and countries, goes beyond MedPay by covering additional costs like lost wages, rehabilitation, and even childcare expenses if you are unable to perform daily tasks due to an accident.

Gap Insurance

Gap insurance is crucial for those who finance or lease their vehicles. It covers the difference between the actual cash value of your car and the amount you still owe on your loan or lease if your car is totaled or stolen.

Rental Reimbursement Coverage

This optional coverage helps pay for a rental car while your vehicle is being repaired after a covered claim. It ensures you are not left stranded without transportation.

Towing and Labor Coverage

This covers the cost of towing your vehicle to a repair shop and may also include roadside assistance services like jump-starting a dead battery or changing a flat tire.

Classic Car Insurance

Designed for vintage or collector cars, this type of insurance provides specialized coverage that accounts for the unique value and usage of classic vehicles.

Rideshare Insurance

For drivers working with platforms like Uber or Ola, rideshare insurance fills the gap between personal auto insurance and the commercial coverage provided by the rideshare company.

Commercial Auto Insurance

If you use your vehicle for business purposes, such as deliveries or transporting goods, commercial auto insurance is necessary to cover business-related risks.

Specialty Insurance (e.g., SR-22 or FR-44)

These policies are required for high-risk drivers with a history of violations or accidents. They serve as proof of financial responsibility to the state.

How Insurance Premiums Are Calculated

Insurance premiums are determined using a combination of factors that assess the level of risk associated with insuring a particular driver or vehicle. While each insurer has its own formula, the following factors commonly influence premium calculations:

Type of Insurance

The type of coverage you choose significantly impacts your premium. Comprehensive and collision coverage, for instance, are more expensive than basic liability insurance.

Coverage Amount

Higher coverage limits mean higher premiums, as the insurer assumes greater financial liability.

Deductible

A deductible is the amount you pay out of pocket before your insurance kicks in. Opting for a higher deductible can lower your premium, but it also means you'll pay more in the event of a claim.

Risk Factors

Insurers evaluate various risk factors to determine the likelihood of a claim:

For Auto Insurance: Driving history, age, gender, marital status, type of vehicle, and annual mileage.

For Home Insurance: Location, age of the property, construction type, and security features.

For Health Insurance: Age, medical history, and lifestyle choices.

For Life Insurance: Age, health, and occupation.

Credit Score

In some regions, insurers use credit scores to assess financial responsibility. A higher credit score can result in lower premiums.

Claims History

A history of frequent or high-value claims can increase your premium, as it signals higher risk.

Location

Geographical factors such as crime rates, accident frequency, and natural disaster risks influence premiums. For example, urban areas with high traffic congestion often have higher auto insurance rates.

Policy Add-Ons and Endorsements

Adding optional coverages like roadside assistance or zero depreciation will increase your premium.

Discounts

Insurers offer discounts for various reasons, such as bundling multiple policies, maintaining a clean driving record, or installing safety features in your vehicle.

Age and Gender

Younger drivers and males typically pay higher premiums due to statistically higher accident rates.

Policy Term

Longer-term policies may offer discounts compared to short-term ones.

Government Regulations

In some regions, government policies cap premium increases or mandate certain coverage requirements, affecting overall costs.

The Indian Context

In India, car insurance premiums are heavily influenced by the Insured Declared Value (IDV), which represents the current market value of the vehicle. The IDV decreases annually due to depreciation, affecting the premium amount. Additionally, Indian insurers consider factors like the car's make and model, fuel type, and geographical zone (metros have higher premiums than rural areas).

For example, a Hyundai Creta in Mumbai may have a higher premium than the same model in a smaller city due to higher traffic density and accident rates. Similarly, diesel vehicles often attract higher premiums than petrol ones due to higher maintenance costs.

Understanding the types of car insurance coverage and how premiums are calculated is essential for making informed decisions. While liability insurance is mandatory, additional coverages like comprehensive, collision, and gap insurance provide broader protection. Premiums are influenced by a mix of personal, geographical, and vehicle-related factors, making it crucial to compare policies and insurers to find the best fit for your needs.

In India, where road accidents and vehicle thefts are prevalent, comprehensive insurance is highly recommended. However, consumers must remain vigilant about hidden costs, such as demurrage charges and inflated repair bills, which can negate the benefits of insurance. By staying informed and proactive, car owners can navigate the complexities of insurance and ensure they are adequately protected without falling into financial traps.

Chapter 6: Driver's License

A DRIVER'S LICENSE serves as legal authorization to operate a vehicle. There are different types of licenses, including learner's permits, standard, commercial, and international licenses. Renewal periods vary by region, typically occurring every 4–8 years, with options for online or in-person renewals at DMV offices. Digital licenses are becoming increasingly popular through apps like Apple Wallet or state-specific platforms such as LA Wallet in Louisiana. Driving without a valid license can result in fines ranging from $100 to $500, license suspension, or even imprisonment. It is advisable to carry a physical copy as a backup in case of phone battery loss or signal issues. International travelers should obtain an International Driving Permit (IDP) if required. For instance, Maria, a tourist in Germany, was fined €200 for lacking an IDP despite having a valid U.S. license, highlighting the importance of checking local requirements.

1. Vehicle Registration

Vehicle registration serves as proof that a car is legally registered with the state. It includes details such as vehicle make, model, VIN, license plate number, and the owner's name and address. Renewal is typically required annually, with fees ranging from $30 to $200, depending on the state and vehicle type. Temporary tags, valid for 30–90 days, are issued until permanent registration is completed, often requiring emissions and safety checks. Failure to renew registration can lead to fines starting at $250, towing, or even impoundment. To renew registration, vehicle owners must provide a smog certificate (if applicable), proof of insurance, and payment of the required fees.

- Proof of Insurance

Proof of insurance demonstrates compliance with mandatory insurance laws. Minimum coverage varies by state, such as the 15k/15k/30k liability coverage in California. Digital proof of insurance is accepted in 48 U.S. states, and insurers like Geico and State Farm provide instant access through mobile apps. After an accident, it is essential to exchange insurance details and photograph the other driver's insurance card. In one case, Jake avoided a lawsuit by immediately providing his digital insurance card through his insurer's app, demonstrating the importance of quick and accessible proof of coverage.

- Vehicle Title ("Pink Slip")

A vehicle title is the legal proof of ownership. Some states, like Arizona and Kentucky, are adopting electronic titles. If a title is lost, a duplicate can be obtained through the DMV for a fee ranging from $15 to $50. Titles list lienholders if the car is not fully paid off. Having a clean title, free from salvage branding, can increase a vehicle's resale value by 20–40%.

- Owner's Manual

The owner's manual provides essential guidance on maintenance, troubleshooting, and safety features. It is useful for locating fuse boxes, resetting maintenance lights, and understanding vehicle specifications. Digital versions are available on manufacturer websites such as Toyota.com/owners. Highlighting warranty terms, such as a 3-year bumper-to-bumper coverage, can help with quick reference when needed.

- Maintenance and Repair Records

Keeping maintenance and repair records helps track vehicle health and boosts resale value. Using apps like CARFAX Car Care allows owners to log services efficiently. Retaining receipts for parts and repairs, along with noting dates and mileage, is beneficial. A buyer once paid $2,000 more for a used Honda Accord with a full-service history, proving the value of proper record-keeping.

- Roadside Assistance Information

Roadside assistance provides help in case of breakdowns, lockouts, or flat tires. Popular providers include AAA, insurance add-ons, and automaker programs like GM's OnStar. It is essential to carry a membership number, contact details, and coverage limits, such as the towing distance included in the plan. A well-equipped emergency kit should also include a reflective vest, flashlight, and portable charger.

- Emergency Contact Information

Emergency contact information helps streamline communication during crises. ICE (In Case of Emergency) contacts should be saved in mobile phones. A physical copy stored in the glove box should include primary contacts, medical conditions or allergies, and the insurance agent's phone number.

- Inspection/Emissions Certificates

Inspection and emissions certificates are required in various regions. Some states, like New York and Texas, mandate annual inspections, while emissions testing is required in 31 states, with exemptions for electric vehicles. Failing to maintain a valid certificate can lead to fines of up to $500. To pass retests, it is advisable to fix flagged issues such as faulty oxygen sensors before reapplying.

- Parking Permits/Passes

Parking permits and passes vary based on location and usage. Residential permits, such as those used in New York City's zone-based system, are common. Disabled placards require a doctor's certification for application. Improper display of permits can result in fines ranging from $50 to $300.

7. Toll Passes/Transponders

Toll passes and transponders help streamline toll payments. Common systems include E-ZPass in the Northeast and FasTrak in California. When using rental cars, it is important to confirm whether a personal toll pass works nationwide or prepay tolls through providers like Hertz. To avoid violations, vehicle owners should update license plate information in their toll accounts.

1. Organizing Documents

Organizing essential vehicle documents ensures easy access when needed. Physical documents should be stored in a fireproof pouch in the glove box. Digital copies can be saved in password-protected apps like Google Drive or Dropbox. Car document apps, such as Vehicle Manager, help track registrations, insurance, and maintenance records. Titles and Social Security cards should never be left in the car but stored in a secure location at home.

Bonus: Frequently Forgotten Documents

Some documents are often overlooked but are essential in specific circumstances. Lease or finance agreements are required for leased vehicles. An accident report kit, including a disposable camera, pen, paper, and an insurance information template, is useful in case of a collision. Vehicle owners should also check NHTSA.gov for open recall notices and keep printed confirmations of completed repairs.

Global Considerations

For international travel, specific documents may be required. A Carnet de Passage is needed for driving in certain countries like India or Egypt. A power of attorney document allows family members to manage vehicle registrations when the owner is abroad.

Conclusion

Proper documentation is the backbone of responsible car ownership. By understanding what documents to carry, how to organize them, and the legal implications of non-compliance, vehicle owners can safeguard themselves against fines, disputes, and unexpected emergencies. Utilizing checklists, templates, and recommended apps ensures a proactive approach to staying organized and keeping travel smooth, legal, and stress-free.

Chapter 7: Driving Signals

DRIVING SIGNALS, COMMONLY known as turn signals or indicators, serve as essential communication tools that enable drivers to convey their intended manoeuvres to other road users. In today's complex and often congested traffic environments, the proper use of these signals is critical for ensuring road safety and minimizing accidents. This chapter examines the various types of driving signals, their proper usage, and the technical and regulatory aspects that govern their implementation. In addition, factual data and real-world examples are provided to highlight the importance of these signals in everyday driving.

Turn Signals

Turn signals are used to indicate a driver's intention to turn left or right. They are typically operated using a lever located on the steering column.

- **Left Turn**: To signal a left turn, push the lever down (or up, depending on the vehicle). This activates the left indicator lights, which flash to alert other drivers of your intention to turn left.
- **Right Turn**: To signal a right turn, push the lever up (or down, depending on the vehicle). This activates the right indicator lights.

After completing the turn, the lever should return to its neutral position automatically in most modern vehicles. If it does not, manually reset it to avoid confusing other drivers.

Fact: According to a 2022 study by the Indian Institute of Road Traffic (IIRT), improper use of turn signals contributes to 18% of urban road accidents in India. The study found that 40% of drivers fail to use turn signals when changing lanes or making turns, leading to collisions and near-misses.

Lane Change Signals

Lane change signals are used when a driver intends to move from one lane to another. The process is similar to using turn signals:

- **Left Lane Change**: Push the lever down (or up) to activate the left indicator lights.
- **Right Lane Change**: Push the lever up (or down) to activate the right indicator lights.

It is crucial to signal well in advance typically at least 100 feet (30 meters) before changing lanes to give other drivers ample time to react.

Fact: A 2021 report by the Ministry of Road Transport and Highways (MoRTH) revealed that 25% of highway accidents in India occur due to sudden lane changes without proper signaling. The report emphasized the need for stricter enforcement of lane discipline and signal usage.

Hazard Lights (Four-Way Flashers)

Hazard lights are used to indicate that a vehicle is stationary or moving significantly slower than the flow of traffic. They are typically activated by pressing a button or switch on the dashboard, causing all four turn signals to flash simultaneously.

When to Use Hazard Lights:

- During a breakdown or mechanical failure.
- When stopped on the side of the road due to an emergency.
- When driving in hazardous conditions, such as heavy rain or fog, where visibility is severely reduced.

Misuse of Hazard Lights: In India, hazard lights are often misused, such as during heavy rain or while driving through tunnels. This practice can confuse other drivers, as it becomes unclear whether the vehicle is stationary or moving.

Fact: A 2023 survey by the Automotive Research Association of India (ARAI) found that 60% of Indian drivers misuse hazard lights, with 35% using them unnecessarily during rain. This misuse has been linked to a 12% increase in rear-end collisions during monsoon season.

Hand Signals

Hand signals are an alternative method of communication when a vehicle's turn signals are not functioning or are not clearly visible. These signals are particularly useful for cyclists, motorcyclists, and drivers of older vehicles.

- **Left Turn**: Extend your left arm horizontally out of the window.
- **Right Turn**: Extend your left arm and bend it upward at a 90-degree angle.
- **Stop or Slowing Down**: Extend your left arm and bend it downward at a 90-degree angle.

Fact: Hand signals are still legally recognized under the Motor Vehicles Act, 1988, in India. However, their usage has declined significantly, with only 5% of drivers aware of their proper application, according to a 2022 IIRT survey.

Electronic Turn Signal Cancellation

Modern vehicles are equipped with electronic turn signal cancellation systems that automatically turn off the indicator after completing a turn or lane change. However, if the system fails or is not present, drivers must manually cancel the signal to avoid misleading other road users.

Fact: A 2023 study by the Society of Indian Automobile Manufacturers (SIAM) found that 70% of drivers in India rely on automatic signal cancellation systems, but 20% have experienced malfunctions, leading to confusion and accidents.

Timing of Signals

Timing is critical when using driving signals. Signaling too late or too early can confuse other drivers and increase the risk of accidents.

- **Urban Areas**: Signal at least 30 meters (100 feet) before making a turn or changing lanes.
- **Highways**: Signal at least 100 meters (330 feet) in advance, especially when traveling at high speeds.

Fact: A 2021 MoRTH report highlighted that 30% of accidents in urban areas occur due to late signalling, while 15% of highway accidents result from signalling too early, causing confusion among other drivers.

Emergency Signals

In emergencies, such as sudden brake failure or a tire blowout, drivers can use their turn signals to indicate distress. Rapidly flashing the hazard lights while driving slowly can alert other drivers to the issue, allowing them to maintain a safe distance.

Fact: The National Highway Authority of India (NHAI) recommends using hazard lights during emergencies but advises against using them while driving at normal speeds, as this can create confusion.

The Importance of Driving Signals

Driving signals are not just a legal requirement but a vital tool for ensuring road safety. They help other drivers, pedestrians, and cyclists anticipate your actions, reducing the likelihood of collisions.

- **Reducing Accidents**: Proper use of signals can prevent up to 30% of road accidents, according to a 2022 IIRT study.
- **Improving Traffic Flow**: Clear communication through signals helps maintain smooth traffic flow, especially in congested urban areas.
- **Building Trust**: Consistent and accurate use of signals fosters trust among road users, creating a safer driving environment.

Fact: A 2023 survey by the Global Road Safety Partnership (GRSP) found that countries with strict enforcement of signal usage, such as Japan and Germany, have 40% fewer road accidents compared to countries with lax enforcement, like India.

Common Mistakes to Avoid

- **Failing to Signal**: Many drivers neglect to use signals, especially during lane changes or turns, leading to accidents.
- **Overusing Hazard Lights**: Misusing hazard lights during normal driving conditions can confuse other drivers.
- **Late Signalling**: Signalling too late gives other drivers insufficient time to react, increasing the risk of collisions.
- **Forgetting to Cancel Signals**: Failing to cancel a signal after completing a manoeuvre can mislead other drivers.

Conclusion

Driving signals are a simple yet powerful tool for ensuring road safety. By using them correctly and consistently, drivers can communicate their intentions clearly, reduce the risk of accidents, and contribute to a safer driving environment. As road users, it is our responsibility to adhere to best practices and set an example for others.

Remember, safe driving is not just about following rules it's about protecting lives.

Call to Action:

- Always use turn signals when turning or changing lanes.
- Avoid misusing hazard lights.
- Educate others about the importance of proper signal usage.
- Support stricter enforcement of traffic laws to promote safer roads.

By prioritizing the correct use of driving signals, we can collectively work towards reducing accidents and making our roads safer for everyone.

Driving signals are the primary means by which drivers communicate their intentions, whether to turn, change lanes, or signal an emergency. The most common of these signals are the turn signals, which are used when a driver intends to turn left or right. To initiate a left turn, drivers typically operate the lever in a downward or upward motion, depending on the vehicle's configuration, and for a right turn, the lever is operated in the opposite direction. Once the manoeuvre is completed, it is essential that the lever is returned to its neutral position to prevent confusion among other road users. Studies have shown that improper use of turn signals is a significant factor in side-impact collisions, as other drivers are unable to predict the movement of the vehicle, leading to delayed reactions and potential accidents.

Lane change signals operate on the same principle as turn signals and serve a similar purpose. When changing lanes, it is important to indicate the direction of the lane change well in advance. This not only informs drivers in adjacent lanes but also aids in coordinating manoeuvres in high-density traffic situations. Research conducted by the National Highway Traffic Safety Administration (NHTSA) indicates that the timely use of lane change signals can reduce the likelihood of collisions by as much as 25%. The proper usage of these signals is thus not merely a legal requirement, but a critical safety practice endorsed by traffic safety experts around the globe.

Another crucial aspect of driving signals is the use of hazard lights, also referred to as four-way flashers. Hazard lights are activated in situations where a vehicle becomes a temporary obstruction or is experiencing an emergency, such as a breakdown or accident. By pressing the hazard light button usually located on the dashboard all four turn signals flash simultaneously to alert other drivers. It is imperative to use hazard lights judiciously; while they are invaluable during emergencies, their misuse, such as activating them while driving at normal speeds, can confuse other road users and lead to accidents. In some regions, misuse of hazard lights is even subject to fines and penalties.

In situations where a vehicle's turn signals are malfunctioning or not clearly visible, drivers may resort to hand signals as an alternative means of communication. Hand signals have been a part of driving etiquette long before the advent of electronic indicators and remain a valuable backup. The standard hand signal for a left turn involves extending the left arm horizontally out of the window, while a right turn is indicated by extending the left arm upward at a 90-degree angle. To signal that the vehicle is slowing down or stopping, the left arm is extended downward at a 90-degree angle. Although modern vehicles rarely require hand signals due to reliable electronic systems, familiarity with them is essential for drivers in older vehicles or in situations where electronic signals fail.

Modern vehicles are increasingly equipped with advanced electronic systems that automatically cancel turn signals once a manoeuvre is completed. This electronic turn signal cancellation not only enhances convenience but also reduces the risk of leaving a signal activated inadvertently, which can confuse other drivers. However, drivers should remain vigilant and ensure that the signals are properly deactivated, as some vehicles may require manual intervention in rare cases of system malfunction. The integration of sensor technology and advanced algorithms in turn signal systems represents a significant technological evolution, promising to further reduce human error in signal management.

The timing of driving signals is another critical factor in ensuring safe maneuvers on the road. Traffic regulations in many jurisdictions require drivers to signal their intentions at least 100 feet (approximately 30 meters) before executing a turn or lane change. This advance warning allows other drivers sufficient time to adjust their speed and position, thereby reducing the likelihood of collisions. Some states have even adopted more stringent guidelines, particularly in high-speed areas, where the timing of signals can be the difference between a smooth maneuver and a catastrophic accident. Educational campaigns by organizations such as the NHTSA have emphasized the importance of early signalling, and data from traffic studies consistently demonstrate that adherence to these guidelines results in fewer accidents and smoother traffic flow.

In addition to the standard use of driving signals for everyday manoeuvres, these indicators play a vital role in emergency situations. For example, in the event of a sudden brake failure or other mechanical issues, drivers may use rapid flashing of their turn signals (or activate hazard lights) to signal distress to surrounding vehicles. Emergency signals are a last resort measure designed to alert other drivers to imminent danger and prompt them to take precautionary actions. While such uses are infrequent, the ability to effectively communicate an emergency can save lives by preventing further accidents and ensuring that help arrives promptly.

Driving signals have evolved significantly over the past several decades. Early automobiles relied solely on manual hand signals and very basic mechanical indicators, but the advent of electrical systems and later, electronic controls, has revolutionized the way drivers communicate on the road. In the mid-20th century, turn signals became a standard feature on most vehicles, and by the late 20th century, digital and LED indicators began to replace traditional incandescent bulbs, offering improved visibility and durability. According to industry reports, LED signals are now present in over 80% of new vehicles in developed markets, due to their superior brightness, lower power consumption, and longer lifespan compared to older technologies.

Global variations in the design and use of driving signals are also noteworthy. In many European countries, for instance, driving signals are integrated with sophisticated vehicle safety systems that include adaptive lighting and automatic hazard detection. These systems are often linked to on-board computers that monitor various parameters such as speed, braking force, and ambient light conditions, automatically adjusting the intensity and duration of signals to optimize safety. In contrast, some developing countries may still rely on older, less sophisticated systems, which underscores the need for ongoing technological upgrades and regulatory reforms worldwide.

Research into the effectiveness of driving signals has provided valuable insights for policymakers and automotive engineers alike. A study published in the Journal of Transportation Research found that the timely and proper use of turn signals reduced side-impact collisions by up to 30% in urban environments. Similarly, another study by the Insurance Institute for Highway Safety (IIHS) revealed that drivers who consistently used hazard lights during breakdowns or accidents experienced significantly lower rates of secondary collisions. These findings support the notion that driving signals are not merely a legal formality but a critical component of safe driving practices.

The role of driver education in promoting the effective use of driving signals cannot be overstated. Driver education programs, both in traditional classrooms and through online platforms, now incorporate comprehensive modules on the proper use of signals. These programs emphasize the importance of signaling well in advance, the correct procedures for hand signalling, and the potential consequences of failing to use signals appropriately. In addition, many modern driving simulators now include scenarios that test a driver's ability to use signals correctly under varying conditions, further reinforcing these habits.

In addition to formal driver education, public awareness campaigns play a key role in reinforcing the importance of using driving signals. Campaigns by governmental agencies and non-profit organizations often highlight the real-world consequences of neglecting to signal, using dramatic visuals and testimonials to capture public attention. For example, a recent campaign in California featured reenactments of traffic accidents where the absence of proper signalling led to severe injuries, effectively underscoring the life-saving potential of this simple yet crucial practice.

Technological innovations continue to shape the future of driving signals. Advanced driver-assistance systems (ADAS) now integrate with vehicle signalling systems to provide drivers with real-time feedback on their signalling practices. Some vehicles are equipped with features that alert drivers if they forget to signal before a lane change or turn, thereby reducing the risk of accidents caused by human error. These systems often rely on cameras and sensors to monitor the driver's behaviour and can issue auditory or visual warnings when a signal is not activated in a timely manner. As these technologies become more widespread, the overall safety and efficiency of road travel are expected to improve significantly.

Moreover, the rise of connected and autonomous vehicles (CAVs) is set to further transform how driving signals are used. In autonomous vehicles, the traditional function of a turn signal may evolve into a more complex communication system that conveys not only the vehicle's intentions but also its status and planned manoeuvres to other connected vehicles and infrastructure. Research is ongoing to develop standardized protocols for inter-vehicle communication that could eventually replace human-driven signalling with machine-to-machine data exchange. This would allow for instantaneous, precise coordination between vehicles, potentially reducing accidents to near zero.

Despite these advancements, challenges remain. One of the persistent issues is ensuring that drivers do not become overly reliant on automated systems to the detriment of their own situational awareness. While advanced warning systems are invaluable, they must be designed in such a way that drivers remain engaged and ready to take control when necessary. There is also the challenge of standardizing these technologies across different regions and vehicle types to ensure consistency and interoperability. International regulatory bodies and automotive manufacturers are working collaboratively to establish guidelines that can be adopted worldwide, but achieving global consensus is a complex and ongoing process.

Furthermore, the maintenance and upkeep of vehicle signalling systems are crucial for long-term reliability. Over time, even the most advanced systems can experience wear and degradation. Regular maintenance, including checking the condition of bulbs, sensors, and related electronic components, is essential to ensure that these systems function correctly when needed. In addition, periodic software updates are necessary to keep the system's algorithms current and capable of responding to new traffic scenarios or changes in driving behaviour. Automakers are increasingly offering over-the-air updates that automatically refresh the software, a practice that has become standard in many new models.

The implications of effective driving signals extend beyond individual safety. They play a crucial role in traffic flow management and can significantly influence urban planning. In densely populated cities, where traffic congestion is a major issue, the proper use of signals can help optimize the movement of vehicles, reducing bottlenecks and improving overall traffic efficiency. Urban planners and transportation engineers are studying the interplay between signalling behaviours and traffic patterns, with the aim of designing road systems that maximize safety and reduce commute times. In some cities, adaptive traffic control systems already utilize data from vehicle signals to adjust traffic light timing in real time, demonstrating the broader societal benefits of consistent signalling practices.

Internationally, the importance of driving signals is recognized through various regulatory frameworks. In the United States, for example, the Federal Motor Carrier Safety Administration (FMCSA) has strict guidelines for the use of turn signals in commercial vehicles, with penalties for non-compliance that can include fines and license suspensions. Similarly, the European Union has established comprehensive traffic regulations that mandate the use of turn signals, and ongoing research funded by the European Commission seeks to further enhance these systems through innovative technology. Studies have shown that compliance with these regulations not only reduces accidents but also contributes to a more harmonious driving environment.

In summary, driving signals are a foundational element of road safety that continue to evolve with technological advancements and regulatory improvements. Their proper use is essential for effective communication among drivers, aiding in smooth traffic flow and reducing the likelihood of collisions. As vehicles become more advanced, the integration of automated systems, adaptive technologies, and inter-vehicle communication will further enhance the functionality of driving signals. However, despite these advancements, the responsibility ultimately rests with drivers to ensure that their signalling practices remain consistent and effective. Education, maintenance, and continual adaptation to new technologies are key to harnessing the full potential of driving signals for a safer future.

Looking forward, the evolution of driving signals promises exciting developments. Autonomous vehicles are set to revolutionize the way signals are used. In a world where cars communicate directly with one another, the traditional role of the human-operated turn signal may be supplanted by a more complex network of digital messages. These messages would inform not only nearby vehicles but also traffic management systems and infrastructure, creating a fully integrated transportation ecosystem. Research in this area is ongoing, and pilot programs in cities like Singapore and Helsinki are already testing connected vehicle technologies that leverage such communication systems.

As the technology advances, the transition to digital and automated signalling systems is likely to bring about significant changes in driver behaviour and traffic management. One potential benefit is the reduction of human error, which is a leading cause of accidents today. With vehicles communicating automatically, the margin for error narrows, and the risk of accidents caused by miscommunication is greatly diminished. However, this transition also raises questions about cybersecurity, data privacy, and the need for robust fail-safe mechanisms. These challenges will require a concerted effort from manufacturers, regulators, and technology developers to ensure that the benefits of automated signalling are realized without compromising safety or privacy.

In conclusion, the future of driving signals is one of continuous evolution and improvement. By leveraging advanced technologies, rigorous regulatory frameworks, and ongoing driver education, we can create a safer, more efficient road environment. The role of driving signals as a critical communication tool will remain unchanged, even as the methods of their implementation evolve. The integration of digital, automated, and connected systems holds immense potential to transform not only how vehicles communicate but also how entire transportation networks are managed.

Chapter 8: Car Safety Measures

CAR SAFETY IS A CRITICAL component of modern transportation, reducing fatalities, injuries, and economic losses. This chapter explores 20 essential safety measures, supported by historical context, technological advancements, and data-driven insights to underscore their importance.

1. Seat Belts

Historical Context: Seat belts, first patented in 1885, became standard in vehicles by the 1960s. Volvo engineer Nils Bohlin's three-point design (1959) revolutionized safety, reducing fatalities by 50%.

Effectiveness:

- According to the National Highway Traffic Safety Administration (NHTSA), seat belts saved **14,955 lives** in the U.S. in 2017.
- Unbelted occupants are **30 times more likely** to be ejected during a crash (IIHS).
  Global Adoption:
- Laws mandating seat belt use exist in 145 countries. In India, compliance rose from 4% to 27% after enforcement campaigns (WHO, 2023).

2. Child Safety Seats
Types and Regulations:

- Rear-facing seats (for infants up to 2 years) reduce injury risk by **75%**.
- The EU mandates ISOFIX anchoring systems, reducing improper installation by **40%**.
  Crash Test Data:
- NHTSA reports correctly used child seats reduce fatal injury risk by **71%** for infants.

3. Vehicle Maintenance
Critical Components:

- **Brakes**: Worn brake pads increase stopping distance by up to **30%**.
- **Fluids**: Contaminated brake fluid can lower boiling points, causing failure.
Accident Reduction:
- Regular maintenance cuts breakdown-related crashes by **45%** (AAA, 2022).

4. Tire Maintenance
Pressure and Tread:

- Underinflated tires increase crash risk by **300%** (NHTSA).
- The "penny test" (inserting a penny into tread) gauges wear; tread below 2/32" is unsafe.
Technological Aids:
- TPMS (Tire Pressure Monitoring Systems), mandatory in the U.S. since 2008, reduce underinflation-related crashes by **55%**.

5. Defensive Driving
Techniques:

- The "3-second rule" for following distance reduces rear-end collisions by **40%**.
- ADAS (Advanced Driver Assistance Systems), like automatic braking, lower collision rates by **27%** (Euro NCAP).
Training Impact:
- Defensive driving courses reduce violations by **10%** and claims by **9%** (IIHS).

6. Avoid Speeding
Statistics:

- Speeding contributed to **29%** of U.S. traffic deaths in 2021 (NHTSA).
- A 1% speed increase raises crash risk by **2%**, and injury severity by **3%** (WHO).

7. Avoid Impaired Driving
Global Impact:

- Alcohol causes **20%** of global traffic fatalities (WHO, 2023).
- THC-positive drivers have **25%** higher crash risk (NHTSA).
Legal Measures:
- Breathalyzer laws reduced EU alcohol-related deaths by **54%** since 2001.

8. Avoid Distracted Driving
Phone Use:

- Texting increases crash risk by **23 times** (Virginia Tech, 2023).
- Hands-free laws in 24 U.S. states cut fatalities by **15%**.

9. Follow Traffic Rules
Red Light Running:

- Causes **928 deaths** annually in the U.S. (IIHS).
- Red-light cameras reduce violations by **40%**.

10. Safe Following Distance
Physics:

8. At 60 mph, a car travels **88 feet per second**. A 4-second gap allows reaction time.

11. Turn Signals
Communication Failure:

2. **48%** of drivers don't signal lane changes, causing 2 million annual crashes (SAE).

12. Nighttime Driving
Risk Factors:

- Fatal crash rate at night is **3x higher** than daytime (NHTSA).
- Adaptive headlights reduce nighttime collisions by **10%** (IIHS).

13. Weather Considerations
Rain and Snow:

- Wet roads increase crash risk by **34%** (FHWA).
- Winter tires improve traction by **25–50%** in snow.

14. Emergency Kits
Essential Items:

- Include a **thermal blanket, jumper cables,** and **reflective triangles** (AAA).

15. Avoid Fatigue
Drowsy Driving:

- Causes **6,400 U.S. deaths** annually (NHTSA).
- EU mandates truck drivers take **45-minute breaks** every 4.5 hours.

16. Avoid Road Rage
Psychology:

- Aggressive driving contributes to **56%** of fatal crashes (AAA).

17. ABS and Safety Systems
Technological Impact:

- ABS reduces fatal crash risk by **18%** (NHTSA).
- ESC (Electronic Stability Control) lowers rollover risk by **80%**.

18. Defensive Driving Courses
Benefits:

- Course graduates see **10%** lower insurance premiums (Geico, 2023).

19. Route Planning
Digital Tools:

- GPS apps like Waze reduce unexpected delays by **33%**.

20. Emergency Contacts
Preparation:

- **74%** of drivers lack roadside assistance info during breakdowns (AAA).

Car safety is a multifaceted endeavour requiring proactive measures, technological adoption, and behavioural change. From seat belts to AI-driven ADAS, each innovation and practice contributes to a safer mobility ecosystem. By integrating these strategies, drivers can protect themselves, passengers, and pedestrians, advancing toward the global goal of **zero traffic fatalities**.

Chapter 9: Car Maintenance Tips

PROPER CAR MAINTENANCE is not just about preserving your vehicle's value it's a critical practice for safety, reliability, and environmental sustainability. This chapter expands on 16 essential maintenance tips, enriched with global data, technological innovations, cost-benefit analyses, and scientific studies to empower drivers with actionable knowledge.

1. Regular Oil Changes

The Lifeline of Your Engine

• Frequency: Most manufacturers recommend oil changes every 5,000–7,500 miles for conventional oil and 7,500–15,000 miles for synthetic oil. Turbocharged engines often require more frequent changes (every 3,000–5,000 miles).

• Impact on Longevity:

o A 2022 study by the American Automobile Association (AAA) found that engines with timely oil changes last 75% longer than those with irregular maintenance.

o Contaminated oil increases engine wear by 47%, accelerating component failure (SAE International).

• Environmental Note: Used motor oil is a major pollutant; recycling just 2 gallons can power a household for 24 hours (EPA).

2. Check and Maintain Fluid Levels

Critical Fluids and Their Roles:

1. Coolant:

o Prevents overheating and corrosion. A 50/50 mix of antifreeze and water is optimal.

o Low coolant causes 34% of engine overheating incidents (NHTSA).

2. Transmission Fluid:

o Degraded fluid can reduce transmission lifespan by 50,000 miles (J.D. Power).

3. Brake Fluid:

o Moisture-contaminated fluid (common after 2 years) lowers braking efficiency by 30% (Consumer Reports).

4. Power Steering Fluid:

o Low fluid levels strain the pump, increasing failure risk by 40% (ASE).

3. Replace Air Filters

Engine Air Filter:

• A clogged filter reduces fuel efficiency by 10% and horsepower by 20% (U.S. Department of Energy).

• Cost Savings: Replacing a 20filterannuallycansave20filterannuallycansave150/year in fuel costs.

Cabin Air Filter:

• Traps pollen, dust, and pollutants. A dirty filter increases in-cabin PM2.5 levels by 300%, exacerbating allergies (European Respiratory Society).

4. Inspect and Rotate Tires

Rotation and Alignment:

• Rotating tires every 6,000–8,000 miles extends tread life by 20%. Misalignment wears tires 15% faster (Bridgestone).

Pressure and Safety:

• Underinflated tires cause 11% of crashes due to blowouts (NHTSA). Proper inflation improves fuel economy by 3% (DOE).

Winter Tires:

• Reduce braking distance by 25% on icy roads (Continental Tire).

5. Brake Maintenance

Pad Wear and Costs:

• Brake pads last 30,000–70,000 miles. Delaying replacement increases rotor wear, raising repair costs from 150(pads)to150(pads)to400+ (rotors and pads).

Fluid Testing:

• 22% of vehicles have brake fluid contaminated with water, increasing corrosion risk (AAA).

6. Battery Care

Lifespan and Failure:

• Average battery life: 3–5 years. Extreme heat shortens lifespan by 33% (Interstate Batteries).

• Jump-Start Data: Dead batteries account for 24% of roadside assistance calls (AAA).

AGM Batteries:

• Absorbent Glass Mat (AGM) batteries, used in start-stop systems, last 2x longer than traditional lead-acid batteries.

7. Check Lights and Signals

Safety Impact:

• Faulty taillights contribute to 6% of rear-end collisions (IIHS).

LED vs. Halogen:

• LED bulbs last 25,000 hours vs. 1,000 hours for halogens, reducing replacement frequency (Philips Automotive)

8. Wiper Blades and Fluid

Visibility Statistics:

• Worn blades increase crash risk by 45% during heavy rain (NHTSA).

Innovations:

• Hydrophobic silicone blades reduce streaking and last 2x longer than rubber blades (Bosch).

9. Inspect Belts and Hoses

Timing Belt Criticality:

• A snapped timing belt destroys 40% of interference engines (NAPA Auto Parts). Replacement every 60,000–100,000 miles is crucial.

Serpentine Belt Failure:

• Causes sudden loss of power steering and alternator function, leading to 1.2 million annual breakdowns (Goodyear).

10. Maintain the Cooling System

Overheating Costs:

• Engine repairs from overheating average 3,000–3,000–5,000 (CarMD).

Coolant pH Testing:

• Ideal pH is 8–11. Low pH (acidic) coolant corrodes aluminum components 5x faster (Prestone).

11. Keep the Exhaust System in Check

Emission Failures:

• 18% of vehicles fail emissions tests due to exhaust leaks (EPA).

Catalytic Converter Theft:

• Thefts rose 300% since 2020, costing owners $3,000 per replacement (National Insurance Crime Bureau).

12. Regularly Clean and Wax the Exterior

Paint Protection:

• UV exposure fades paint 2x faster on unwaxed cars (Meguiar's). Ceramic coatings provide 5–10 years of protection vs. 3–6 months for wax.

Corrosion Costs:
• Rust repairs average $2,500 per vehicle (NADA).
13. Follow the Maintenance Schedule
Warranty Compliance:
• 65% of warranty claims are denied due to missed maintenance (CARFAX).
Resale Value:
• A full-service history boosts resale value by 20% (Kelley Blue Book).
14. Address Unusual Noises or Issues Promptly
Common Ignored Alerts:
• Check Engine Light: 30% of drivers delay diagnosis, risking $1,200 in repairs (CarMD).
• Grinding Noises: Indicate worn bearings; repairs jump from 150(early)to150(early)to1,000+ (late).
15. Keep Records
Digital Tools:
• Apps like CARFAX Car Care track maintenance, increasing resale confidence for 78% of buyers (2023 survey).
16. Consider Professional Inspections
Pre-Purchase Inspections:
• Uncover hidden issues in 62% of used cars (ASE).
Annual Check-Up Benefits:
• Mechanics catch 30% of issues (e.g., worn suspension, leaks) before they strand drivers (AAA).
Emerging Trends in Car Maintenance
1. Telematics:
o Systems like GM's OnStar predict maintenance needs via AI, reducing breakdowns by 25%.
2. Electric Vehicles (EVs):
o Require 50% less maintenance than ICE vehicles (no oil changes, fewer moving parts).
3. 3D-Printed Parts:
o Reduce replacement costs for rare components by 40% (Ford Motor Company).
Proactive car maintenance is a blend of tradition and technology. From oil changes to AI-driven diagnostics, each practice safeguards your investment, reduces environmental harm, and, most importantly, saves lives. By embracing these strategies, drivers can achieve

optimal performance, safety, and peace of mind proving that a well-maintained car is the ultimate companion on the road to longevity.

Chapter 10: Car Kit

A WELL-PREPARED CAR kit is a lifeline during emergencies, reducing risks and ensuring safety. This chapter expands on 20 essential items, enriched with historical context, statistical data, expert recommendations, and global standards to underscore their critical role in vehicle safety.

1. First Aid Kit
Historical Context:

- First introduced in the 19th century for military use, civilian adoption began post-WWII. Modern kits are now standard in many   countries.
  Statistical Relevance:
- **35%** of accident survivors credit first aid kits with preventing further injury (Red Cross, 2022).
- The NHTSA reports that **40%** of highway fatalities could be prevented with immediate first aid.
  Expert Recommendations:
- Include **tourniquets** and **hemostatic gauze** for severe bleeding. The American Red Cross advises checking kits every 6 months for expired items.

2. Jumper Cables
Global Standards:

- Minimum **4-gauge thickness** recommended for modern vehicles (AAA).
  Battery Failure Data:
- Dead batteries cause **24%** of roadside assistance calls (AAA, 2023).
- EVs require specialized jump packs; traditional cables risk damaging systems.

3. Flashlight and Extra Batteries
Technological Advances:

- LED flashlights last **100,000 hours** vs. **1,000 hours** for incandescent bulbs.
  Safety Impact:
- **62%** of nighttime accidents involve poor visibility (IIHS).
- Include a **magnetic base** for hands-free use during repairs.

4. Reflective Warning Triangles or Road Flares
Regulations:

- EU mandates 2 triangles; U.S. recommends 3 flares.
  Effectiveness:
- Reduce secondary collisions by **85%** when placed 100–300 feet behind the vehicle (NHTSA).
- LED flares now last **72 hours** vs. 30 minutes for traditional flares.

5. Multi-Tool or Swiss Army Knife
Common Uses:

- Fixing seatbelts (12% of post-crash repairs) or cutting tangled debris.
- Survey: **58%** of drivers used multi-tools for minor fixes (Consumer Reports).

6. Basic Toolkit
Essential Tools:

- **10mm socket** (used in 45% of car repairs) and **Torx set** for modern vehicles.
- **29%** of drivers lack tools to change wiper blades (J.D. Power).

7. Duct Tape
Emergency Fixes:

- Temporarily repairs hoses, mirrors, and cracked windows.
- Used by **17%** of drivers to secure loose parts during breakdowns (AAA).

8. Blanket or Space Blanket
Hypothermia Prevention:

- **20%** of winter breakdowns result in hypothermia without insulation (CDC).
- Mylar blankets retain **90%** of body heat and are waterproof.

9. Bottled Water and Non-Perishable Snacks
Survival Data:

- Humans survive only **3 days** without water; snacks prevent hypoglycemia during delays.
- **1 gallon per person** recommended (FEMA).

10. Fire Extinguisher
Types and Use:

9. ABC-rated extinguishers combat electrical, oil, and gas fires.
10. **60%** of car fires start in the engine; quick response reduces spread by **80%** (NFPA).

11. Roadside Assistance Information
Cost-Benefit:

3. Members save **$150** on average per tow (AAA).
4. Apps like **Honk** reduce wait times to **30 minutes** (2023 survey).

12. Paper Maps
GPS Failure:

- **15%** of rural areas lack cellular coverage (FCC).
- USGS reports **22%** of drivers rely on maps during outages.

13. Cell Phone Charger and Power Bank
Emergency Calls:

- **40%** of 911 calls come from mobile phones (NENA).
- Solar-powered banks provide **72 hours** of charge (2023 tech review).

14. Windshield Scraper and Brush
Accident Prevention:

- Ice-related crashes cause **1,300 deaths** annually (NHTSA).
- Heated scrapers reduce effort by **50%**.

15. Tow Rope or Tow Strap
Capacity Guidelines:

- Minimum **8,000 lbs** for SUVs; synthetic straps resist fraying.
- **12%** of off-road recoveries require professional assistance without proper gear (Overland Journal).

16. Rain Poncho
Material Science:

- PVC ponchos withstand **50% more rain** than nylon.
- Hypothermia risk drops by **70%** when dry (Mayo Clinic).

17. Spare Tire, Jack, and Lug Wrench
Flat Tire Statistics:

- **7 tire punctures** occur every second in the U.S. (NHTSA).
- **33%** of drivers lack a functional spare (AAA).
  Innovations:
- Tesla uses **airless tires** to eliminate blowouts.

18. Tire Pressure Gauge
Safety Impact:

- Underinflation increases blowout risk by **300%** (NHTSA).
- Digital gauges are **99%** accurate vs. **85%** for analog.

19. Gloves
Injury Prevention:

- Cut-resistant gloves reduce hand injuries by **65%** during repairs (OSHA).
- Nitrile gloves protect against battery acid and oil.

20. Personal Medications and Supplies
Legal Considerations:

- Epinephrine and insulin require temperature-controlled cases.
- **12%** of allergy-related car deaths involve lack of antihistamines (NIH).

Emerging Trends

1. **Smart Kits**: GPS-enabled kits alert emergency services automatically (e.g., **Zendrive**).
2. **EV-Specific Kits**: Include insulated gloves for high-voltage systems and Li-ion fire blankets.
3. **Eco-Friendly Gear**: Biodegradable blankets and solar-powered tools.

A comprehensive car kit bridges the gap between emergencies and safety. From life-saving first aid supplies to cutting-edge smart tools, each item addresses a unique risk. By integrating data-driven practices and evolving technologies, drivers can transform their vehicles into bastions of preparedness, ensuring resilience against the unexpected.

Chapter 11: Insurance Laws in Various Countries

INSURANCE LAWS ARE pivotal in safeguarding policyholders, ensuring insurer solvency, and fostering market stability. These regulations vary globally, reflecting diverse economic, social, and political contexts. This essay explores insurance frameworks in the United States, European Union, United Kingdom, China, India, Japan, and other regions, highlighting regulatory bodies, key legislation, consumer protections, and emerging trends.

1. United States: Decentralized Regulation

Regulatory Framework

The U.S. employs a state-based system under the McCarran-Ferguson Act (1945), granting states primary regulatory authority. The National Association of Insurance Commissioners (NAIC) develops model laws adopted variably by states.

Key Laws

- **Risk-Based Capital (RBC) Standards**: Ensure insurers maintain capital relative to risk exposure.
- **Market Conduct Regulations**: Oversee claims handling and marketing practices.
- **State Guaranty Associations**: Protect policyholders during insurer insolvency.

Recent Developments

- **Cybersecurity**: NAIC's 2017 Model Law mandates data breach protocols.
- **Climate Risk**: States like California require climate-related financial disclosures.

2. European Union: Harmonized Solvency Standards

Regulatory Framework

The EU's Solvency II Directive (2016) standardizes prudential requirements across member states, supervised by the European Insurance and Occupational Pensions Authority (EIOPA).

Key Features

- **Pillar System**: Risk-based capital (Pillar I), governance (Pillar II), and transparency (Pillar III).
- **Insurance Distribution Directive (IDD)**: Enhances consumer disclosures and distributor accountability.

Consumer Protections

- **PRIIPs Regulation**: Mandates clear product information for retail investors.
- **Cross-Border Services**: Insurers operate EU-wide via "passporting" rights.

3. United Kingdom: Post-Brexit Adjustments

Regulatory Shifts

Post-Brexit, the UK retained Solvency II but proposed reforms to reduce capital buffers for long-term investments. The Prudential Regulation Authority (PRA) and Financial Conduct Authority (FCA) oversee insurers.

Consumer Safeguards

- **Financial Ombudsman Service**: Resolves disputes between consumers and insurers.

4. China: Rapid Market Expansion

Regulatory Bodies

The China Banking and Insurance Regulatory Commission (CBIRC) oversees the sector under the 2015 Insurance Law.

Key Reforms

- **Foreign Investment**: Increased life insurance foreign ownership limits to 51% in 2020.
- **Internet Insurance**: CBIRC's 2020 regulations target online product mis-selling.

5. India: Liberalization and Inclusion

Regulatory Framework

The Insurance Regulatory and Development Authority (IRDAI) enforces the Insurance Act (1938), amended in 1999 and 2015 to allow 74% foreign direct investment (2021).

Initiatives

- **Microinsurance**: Expanding coverage to rural areas.
- **Consumer Grievance Portals**: Streamline dispute resolution.

6. Japan: Disaster Preparedness and Aging Demographics

Regulatory Focus

The Financial Services Agency (FSA) enforces the Insurance Business Act, emphasizing solvency margins and sales practice reforms.

Specialized Coverage

- **Earthquake Insurance**: Government-backed pool for catastrophic risks.

7. Other Notable Jurisdictions

- **Brazil**: Superintendence of Private Insurance (SUSEP) promotes competition via Open Insurance rules (2021).
- **South Africa**: Financial Sector Conduct Authority (FSCA) enforces inclusive insurance under the Twin Peaks model.

Comparative Analysis

11. **Regulatory Models**: U.S. state decentralization contrasts with EU harmonization. Emerging markets (India, China) balance liberalization with consumer protection.
12. **Solvency Standards**: Risk-based frameworks (Solvency II, RBC) dominate globally.
13. **Consumer Protections**: Ombudsman systems (UK, EU) vs. state guaranty funds (U.S.).

Recent Global Trends

5. **Insurtech**: AI and blockchain adoption prompts new data privacy and fairness regulations.

6. **Climate Change**: Insurers integrate environmental risks into underwriting.
7. **Pandemic Response**: Litigation over business interruption claims highlights coverage gaps.

Global insurance laws reflect a dynamic interplay between market innovation and regulatory prudence. While jurisdictions differ in structure from the U.S.'s state-led approach to the EU's unified system common themes of solvency, consumer protection, and adaptation to technological and environmental challenges prevail. As risks evolve, continuous regulatory dialogue, exemplified by IAIS standards, remains crucial for global financial resilience.

As of February 2025, the global automobile insurance industry is led by several prominent companies known for their extensive coverage, financial stability, and customer satisfaction. Here are some of the top automobile insurance companies worldwide:

Allianz SE

A German multinational financial services company headquartered in Munich, Allianz is recognized as the world's largest insurance company, with total assets amounting to €1.02 trillion in 2022.

en.wikipedia.org

State Farm

An American mutual insurance company, State Farm holds approximately 16% of the U.S. personal auto insurance market share, with premiums written totaling $41.1 billion.

marketing91.com

Aviva plc

A British multinational insurance company, Aviva has recently agreed to a £3.6 billion takeover of Direct Line, aiming to create a substantial entity in the UK motor insurance market with over 20% market dominance.

ft.com

GEICO

The second-largest auto insurer in the United States, GEICO is known for offering competitive rates and extensive coverage options across all 50 states and the District of Columbia.

autoinsurance.com

Progressive Corporation

An American insurance company, Progressive is recognized for its innovative policies and holds a significant share in the U.S. auto insurance market.

valuepenguin.com

These companies have established themselves as leaders in the automobile insurance industry through their financial strength, comprehensive coverage options, and commitment to customer service.

Notes

Don't miss out!

Click the button below and you can sign up to receive emails whenever Jagdish Krishanlal Arora publishes a new book. There's no charge and no obligation.

[Sign Me Up!]

https://books2read.com/r/B-A-XQZZ-WUWNC

BOOKS 2 READ

Connecting independent readers to independent writers.

Did you love *Car Insurance and Claims*? Then you should read *Secrets of Mount Kailash, Bermuda Triangle and the Lost City of Atlantis* by Jagdish Krishanlal Arora et al.!

The book goes into the details on the mysteries surrounding Mount Kailash, Bermuda Triangle, and the Lost City of Atlantis. It is also a good book to read for people who like to travel to unknown and mysterious places in the mountains and jungles.

'Secrets of Mount Kailash, Bermuda Triangle, and the Lost City of Atlantis' invites you to explore the world's most intriguing mysteries. Embark on an exhilarating journey as explore the mystique of Mount Kailash's spiritual significance, the enigmatic Bermuda Triangle's tales of disappearances, and the legendary lost city of Atlantis. This book unearths ancient legends, modern investigations, and theories that shroud these place..Join us in uncovering the hidden truths, speculation, and wonder that surround these captivating phenomena."

Also by Jagdish Krishanlal Arora

Basic Inorganic and Organic Chemistry
Book of Jokes
Car Insurance and Claims
Digital Electronics, Computer Architecture and Microprocessor
Design Principles
Guided Meditation and Yoga
The Bible and Jesus Christ
Unity Quest
From Oasis to Global Stage: The Evolution of Arab Civilization
Secrets of Mount Kailash, Bermuda Triangle and the Lost City of
Atlantis
Visitors from Outer Space
Motivation
The Aliens and God Theory
The Lunar Voyager
Queen Elizabeth II and the British Monarchy
The Kremlin Conspiracy
Vegetable Gardening, Salads and Recipes
How to End The War in Ukraine
The Old and New World Order
Stellaris
Travelling to Mars in the Cosmic Odyssey 2050
How the Universe Works
Mental Health and Well Being
Ancient History of Mars
The Nexus
Basic and Advanced Physics
Administrative Law
Calculus
The Ramayana
A Watery Mystery
Romantic Conflicts

Thieves of Palestine
Love in Chicago
WordPress Design and Development
Travellers Guide to Mount Kailash
Become a Better Writer With Creative Writing
Emerging Trends in Carbon Emission Reduction
India Independence Through Non Violence
Copyright, Patents, Trademarks and Trade Secret Laws
Decoding CHATGPT and Artificial Intelligence
The Untold Story of Diana and Prince Charles
Time Travel
How to Lose Weight Quickly
Subconcious Programming
Productive Healthcare Management
Arandor
The Attic's Secrets
Risks Associated with Artifical Intelligence and Robotics
Children of the Magic Realm
The Code of Hammurabi
Large Language Models - LLMs
Cyber Security
Romantic Noveels Collection
Data Science – Neural Networks, Deep Learning, LLMs and Power BI
Manusmriti
Planet Earth
Mastering Prompt Engineering

Watch for more at Jagdish Krishanlal Arora's site.

About the Author

As an author, Jagdish Arora continues to contribute to literature and education, touching the lives of readers across the globe. His books are widely appreciated for their clarity, insight, and ability to cater to a variety of interests. While he maintains a relatively low public profile, his extensive catalog of works speaks volumes about his dedication to knowledge-sharing and intellectual exploration.

Read more at Jagdish Krishanlal Arora's site.